Bishop,

This book is my first big project and I'm so happy that I'm sharing this with you. I pray this book opens up a new experience with God. That it creates wonderful God moments and fill in the cracks in your foundation. I love you man of God with all I am as a woman. You truly are a gift from God. Therefore focus, begin again fill in your four dots, and win

Your Wife
First Lady Mitchell
❤ 5-4-22

AS YOU WERE....
FIRST LADY COLLECTION
A NEW NORMAL

VOLUME ONE

Created and written By
TINA LOUISE MITCHELL
Foreword by Bishop Milano T. Mitchell

authorHOUSE

AuthorHouse™
1663 Liberty Drive
Bloomington, IN 47403
www.authorhouse.com
Phone: 833-262-8899

Published by AuthorHouse 03/15/2022

ISBN: 978-1-6655-5339-1 (sc)
ISBN: 978-1-6655-5338-4 (e)

CONTENTS

FOREWORD

FROM THE DESK OF BISHOP MILANO T. MITCHELL....

If you ever desired to be free from anything, even yourself. Here is a great read from a dynamic woman of God, who has endured the lows of life and have come through the fire to become one of life's and God's greatest soldiers. Follow along as my wife deals with self-sabotage and takes strong accountability measures.

May God bless you on your journey.

Sincerely,

INTRODUCTION

Throughout Tina Mitchell's life she found herself faced with many unforeseen distractions that led to dark seasons and because of this, she proposed in her heart to become a beacon of light to help those that are lost in their own darkness. The darkness that life can cause within one's heart and mind after tragedy strikes.

From losing most of her family to untimely deaths; to birthing a special needs child with severe medical challenges; to losing a 22 year old son abruptly; to falling victim to an unexpected crack addiction; to an exhausting uphill battle for love; to fighting to win her children back from the state; to being one of the most gossiped about first ladies; she'll capture you with her undying commitment to God, her humbling look at life, and her relentless love for God's people.

Come go along with her as she recalls these powerful moments and create new amazing memories.

In this series of books you'll read how God showed First Lady Tina how not just to come up out of sin, but how to submit wholly to God.

Each book will share with you how the First Lady found out who she is, whose she is, and who God is through her.

Dynamic seasons of life filled with God's presence and provision, the Holy Spirit's leading, miracles and faith. Search the scriptures with the First Lady as she finds her inner strength and faith in God to root out generational curses embedded in her lineage, destroy them, and maintain victory

Each short read is a step closer to wholeness and you can rest assured that they will keep you in suspense while creating a new outlook on life....

Come and be blessed....Your life will never be the same

A LETTER FROM THE FIRST LADY....

I put in the hard work to see the ugliness in me to be an example of change to all who need to see one. It is my desire to give you the tools to help start a wildfire of spiritual success in your life. I pray my experiences encourage your faith to boldly pick up wherever you left off in fulfilling your purpose in life.

My Loves.... focus, begin again, fill in your four dots and win.

As you were....

First Lady 💋

DEDICATIONS

This book is dedicated to My Lord and Savior **Jesus Christ** because without the cross I never would have had the opportunity to get it right. I cannot imagine anyone with more do overs than me. You truly are my heart's desire because when it's all over it's just me and you.

To My dear sweet husband **Bishop Milano T Mitchell**, You are the epitome of a good husband and a Great Man of God. I am so blessed that you found me. I love you and how you love me.

To **Bishop Marvin L Winans** thank you for staying in place. My mom found her rest knowing we were in good hands. Love you Pastor

To **Bishop Andrew Merritt and Pastor Vicky**, thank you for imparting the spirit of excellence in me. It is truly an honor and privilege to be one of your children. Love you eternally

To **Bishop and Apostle Blacksher(PawPaw and TT)**, Thank you for every word, prayer, moment, late night ear, smile and tear. You truly are irreplaceable. I love you both to life.

To My Momma **Sharon,** They don't make 'em like you anymore You are my mother. I love you.

To My Sister **Norma**, I just love you period. Thank you for how you are with me.

To My Brother **Britt,** You are everything I never knew I needed in a brother. Love you

To each and every one of **My remaining children** both naturally and spiritually

I am so thankful to be your mom. I pray God's best, God's will and God's way for your lives.

I love you (**GeorgeIII,MarlinII,Destiny,Joshua,Christina,and Elijah**)(Natasha,Renee,Mya)

(Aliyah,Ashanti,MilanoJr)(Darius,Brandon,Faith,CJ,Krystal,Lunden, Brianna,Donae,Angel,Jasmine,Nakia)

To my family in its entirety, There isn't enough paper to tell you how honored I am to be a part of some of the kindest, talented, anointed, loving, gangsta folk this side of glory. I love you all to life.

Now in loving memory of... My Kuipiio Livingston, there will never be another you for me.

My Dad, My Mom, My brothers, My sisters, My uncles, My aunties, My nieces, My nephews, My cousins, My grandparents, My best friends, My first loves, My mentors, but most importantly My children who have gone on to be with the Lord especially **Nathan** Charles, **Denise** G'Kema, and My **Kevin** Wilson, until we meet again.

If I've forgotten anyone, charge it to my age and not my heart.

Love you 2, First Lady☺

Tina,
You have more good left

than the good you lost...

It's the spring of 2016, I'm sitting on the side of my bed hearing this familiar sound, sounds like a wounded animal.

Where did I hear that sound before and where is it coming from?

Oh, my God! It's getting louder!!! What is it??? Make it stop!!!

Please, make it stop… hold on one minute, is that???...

Is that ME???..... IT'S ME!!! WHAT IS GOING ON???

My head is pounding. My heart is aching. My womb is throbbing.

It then dawned on me that I was returning from my mind wandering off. I was daydreaming again but I'm back now, back to my present state, back to what I thought to be a horrible existence.

Back to the reality that my second born, my 9 days shy of 23 years old Kevin is gone. My peanut butter loving, Michael Jackson moonwalk dancing, long word quoting, brillant, cool, all around great guy Kevin….. He's gone???.

My son, my gift from God, my little man, my baaaaaabbbyyyyy.... He's Goooooooone, Killed.... Dead.

I'm at my lowest in my life and it's about to mark a year of this terrible event that forever changed me.

The image flashed like lightning, the impact of the driver's car hitting my son's bike with such force that it impaled him and totally shattered his pelvis . I'm now fully aware that the sound I'm hearing is me. It's me sobbing so ferociously that it is bellowing a low bone shaking moan, accompanied by an unheard gut wrenching scream from my soul. A true agonizing groan from the core of my being. From an emptiness trapped in an abyss that's darkest of all blackness. Life had touched me and I was frozen drenched in pain and fear, trembling and crying. Afraid that if I moved I would lose all control and everything I had left.

Did I have anything left....Why couldn't I just die.......

This is the tornado chapter

A tornado is defined as a person or thing characterized by violent or devastating action or emotion. That can *summarize*

(***give a brief statement of the main points of***) this particular season in my life. The season I lost Kevin was filled with devastating actions and emotions. When you love someone you do not allow them to just die or give in to death. And thank God, God loved me enough not to let me die in that season.

When my son passed away, I thought that I turned my back on God because I was trying to be disqualified from the big trials. I thought maybe losing my son was a, "Have you considered my servant Tina?" challenge for the enemy. I felt much like Job in the Old Testament of the Bible (The book of Job). I was seemingly minding my own business and all of hell broke loose in my life.

I thought if I did enough bad God wouldn't want me anymore.

I was so wrong, God softly said, "I don't change my mind." I wish I knew that before I started all those bad habits up again. Sitting realizing that I had made my life worse with bad habits, I asked God, " How can I even come out of this?" He lovingly said," Tina, You have more good left than the good you lost." I just began to cry.

God thought that what I lost was good, how could anyone think more of Kevin than me. How could God think Kevin was good and let him be taken like that? Oh how my thinking has changed so much since then. God referred to Kevin as my good. God could have said I had more left than what I lost but He specifically referred to him as good. It let me know then that God cared about what was important to me.

There are countless stories in the books of the gospel (Books of Matthew, Mark, Luke, and John) where ordinary people much like you and I went to Jesus on behalf of people they loved and Jesus was human with them. Jesus even marveled at the fact that their love fed their faith in Him as Christ the Messiah. That just goes to show Jesus cares about what concerns us, because it leads to His glory. God lovingly told me I had more good left than the good I lost. Irecall thinking, what could I possibly have left that was good after losing My Kevin?

I was so out of it and still functioning….. I just couldn't see it, pain clouded my vision and every inch of me hurted. It hurted to move, to think, to breathe, to live. It was so bad, I was in a void without light or air. I remember God lit a match and sat down in it with me. It was darker than black but I saw a glimmer of hope.

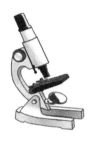

Embracing My

"New Normal"

This is the microscope chapter.

A microscope is used to examine objects that are too small to be seen by the naked eye. Coming into the awareness of my new normal without Kevin was gonna take more than what could be seen on the surface. Assessing where I was at was hard because by the time the smoke cleared from my son's death I was on autopilot. My very existence was working overtime from every past season and experience in my life, good and bad.

My entire life was a rollercoaster, from being born a Pastor's daughter in a dysfunctional single parent home growin up to marry, to touring as an entertainer. Living an absolutely amazing celebrity life only to become a two time divorcee. And let's not forget the happy go lucky naive child deep down that secretly loved to worship and preach, talking about confusion.....

Everything in me came out to save me when I shut down on life After Kevin died. I was comatosed, too traumatized to feel the basic emotions and I was trapped inside of me with all those people. How did I get there?

Looking back I remember sitting at Kevin's bedside after he had passed, picturing my heart in my hand and it running through my fingers like sand. I whispered, "God, If I didn't know you loved me I would swear you hated me." I know now it was then that I shut God out and began to side-eye His every move. I lost my hope and I let the enemy have my mind because I was tired of thinking, I was tired of fighting, I was tired of loving, and I was tired of living. and so it began....

Over the next year I just let myself go to sin to attempt to self medicate my pain. I heard everyone like I was in a bubble and responded to everything from memory. I didn't know how to live and process time. I had lost my instinct to see something, think and respond. I was struggling so I voiced my desire to die to everyone that would hear until my oldest son finally said, "The younger children aren't the only ones that need you." I stopped saying it out loud but I couldn't stop thinking about it. I wanted out by whatever means necessary.

I don't know how, but I know it had to be God that began to show me the good I had left. I had my children and I had a special friend I met online that would always minister to me and have me sing to him. It's something how his voice was the only voice that didn't sound distorted. He later became instrumental in my deliverance.

A few months after the year anniversary of Kevin's death, I dropped the last load of my packed up things off at a storage unit, packed my remaining 6 children up in my GMC Envoy and left what I always knew as home, Detroit Michigan. Trying to run from the pain of losing my son I dove head first into the most tumultuous journey I had ever been on in my entire life.

Something deep down in me drove me away, like wild horses. The force behind me drove me away from Detroit like bats out of the pit of hell, little did I know with that same force I was being catapulted into what was under the surface?

En route to Florida, I stopped and made St Louis my home. I thought I stopped here because my son was stationed in the army here. Or maybe my online friend was here and was my help. It even came to mind this was the furthest I had lived from all my family in Detroit and I did not want to drive any further. However none of those were why I ended up here. Why did I come here then?

Constant

Crossroads

This is the compass chapter

A compass can be defined as a device having a magnetic needle that indicates direction on the earth's surface by pointing toward the north. Growing up, I always knew north to be up and south to be down. Isn't it something how a compass is designed to show you where you are based on where up is.

Moving to St. Louis, Missouri from Detroit, Michigan was geographically moving south(down) but spiritually I declare it was moving up, because I moved closer to God than I had ever been before In my life.

So you see I found that I was brought down here to make a choice without personal influences. Like when God told Abraham to leave his family In the first Book of the Bible. (Genesis)

Throughout my life I've always come to constant crossroads. There were always obvious choices before me in my life to either choose God's way or the world's way. Relationships, careers, even as far as me being a student of the arts.

Loving to act and sing when the opportunity was presented to do a full movie and to record a whole album you'd think I'd jump at it but I passed because they wanted me to be a pied piper figure and come out in a secular genre.

I understand it now but then I was too fearful of the accessibility of temptations. But as quiet as kept I could have gone that way, because all of the things I ran from, my own instincts ran me straight into anyway. I'll touch on that in the unavoidable purpose chapter.

This was one of the many times I purposely chose God over fame and fortune. And it wasn't because I didn't want it because most of my life it was all I wanted outside of Jesus.

Not now but in times past, I constantly struggled with financial bondage but had more than enough talents, character, morals, ethics, wisdom, and faith. To be honest, a lot of times a truckload of hard cash would have been an easy fix. Don't get me wrong God is absolutely amazing when it comes to provision.

God provided handsomely with unexpected income and favor when it came to me, and still to date. I've been told many times, I receive more unexpected income than anyone these people knew. I can recall time after time monies being put on my debit cards and bills paid anonymously. Too many to count throughout my life. That brings me to my last, how would I put it, test of faith.

The fall of 2020, I had the choice to follow more money than ever before or God and I followed God. I thank God for second chances because my decision led to me marrying the man of my dreams. God had ordered our steps back to one another, I'm forever grateful.

However, If I had to make that same decision a year before it may be slightly different because conditions were so different for me. I was heavily addicted to crack cocaine. What a difference a year makes? I had totally let the enemy wreak havoc in my mind and one substance led to another. For so long my life no longer resembles anything I could have ever remembered it to be.

From February 2015 to June of 2020 I spiraled totally out of control. I had accumulated warrants for my arrest, lost my children to the state, lost almost 100 pounds and lost any sense of a healthy image of myself. And it all started from trying to forget my son's death. I didn't think that plan through, AT ALL!!!!!.

So by the fall, I was coming out of that nightmare, I had begun to have overnight visits with the children, I was having constant clean drug drops, I was gaining weight and really hearing God clear. What could cause such a drastic transformation? And what can I say led to my deliverance?

The key was to MAKE THE DECISION to do good. And to begin choosing actions that only supported doing good. The more I submitted the easier.The blessings and power that comes from choosing to do good are indescribable. Now please know that you can choose to do right and NOT immediately start doing good.

The Apostle Paul walks us through the will to do good and the fight to do good in the New Testament of the Bible. (the Book of Romans Chapters 7 and 8)

Scriptures fine tune our spiritual compass. The bible says Seek ye first the kingdom of God and His righteousness and your necessities are added. (Matthew 6:33) And in another place it says that God is a rewarder of those that continuously seek Him. (Hebrews 11:6)

This means our spiritual compasses are like treasure maps, they always have a treasure at the end of the journey. Whether short or long, there is always a reward. Some great, some small but all necessary to fulfill our purpose. Don't you want to know why you were born? It couldn't just be to live. My life wasn't just to keep landing on my feet.

All of this wisdom and insight did not drop on me overnight but it took years of making mistakes, wanting to get it right, abandonments, betrayals, let downs, insults, lies, unnecessary trips around the same mountains, self righteousness, denial, laziness, intentionally and unintentional falls and some.

And with all of that happening I still didn't just start abusing drugs. When I began to side-eye God, note that that was my new normal. I had lost confidence in my lifeline and I had begun to die, spiritually.

My self medicating created an appetite that led to a lust that drew me away as illustrated in the new testament of the Bible. (James 1:14). In a nutshell everything was done in steps.

A Lean Life

This is the checklist chapter

A checklist is a list of items required, things to be done, or points to be considered, used as a reminder. When I look back at my failures I can see the obvious steps to destruction. I recognized what type of people I kept around, what dangers I entertained, what spiritual weather conditions it took, what posture to stand in and what language was most important.

When my son Kevin first passed away the people around me immediately began to change. Some that were grounded in Christ walked away, and some that were lost began to flock to me. I felt like David in the cave of Adullam as in The Old Testament of the Bible (The book of I Samuel 22:1-2). I remember being so strong right after for everyone hurting and then the smoke cleared and I fell completely apart. You hear me?!? APART!!!

Man, you could not have even imagined the surprise at my total turn around. From a great woman of God, serving the lord with gladness to a yet again broken backslider. I would have at least responded from surprise and got back up after such a great loss. But I was too busy trying to ignore the obviously bigger pain to settle for the *minute* (**very small or of small importance**) pain of pity.

To be honest, it just felt easier to bear. I couldn't look the loss of my son in the eyes. I was as the older folk said, I was shamefaced. I felt exposed and naked. Such a degrading place, I felt like I was groveling to life. It was pathetic if I do say so myself. Pathetic and just the right conditions to groom me for a horrible drug addiction. The pity was to lure me, to take my hand and walk me right into danger. To lullaby me into an *alter* **(to make different without changing into something else)** existence

The plan was not just to take me off course but to have me abort my whole mission entirely. These are some of the things that take place to lead you to sin. Your details may not be my specifics, but the luring feels the same. Do you see yourself? Or similar conditions that led or are leading you away from God?

Check-in, where are you today? Where is your mind? What are you thinking about the most? Do you focus on failures or in spite of life's setbacks, you continually praise God for your many blessings? Take a moment to think about this moment in your life. Write down what's going on right now in your life whether good or bad. Do that and come back.... (take a small break)

Okay now, I pray you did it. .I want you to do a little project. For everything that's weighting on your heart, write a confession that you're believing it to become.

Can you begin to say it everyday? It can just be as simple as, "I will come out of this." Try it and write to me so I can pray with you. My email is firstladytinamitchell@gmail.com.

Put **Attn: Prayer Requests** in the subject box. Okay, let's continue.

Some of the things that were on the list leading to my using drugs included being depressed, losing hope, talking negative, hanging with people that were already abusing, shutting God out, allowing negative thoughts to flood my mind, believing the enemy, not pressing into prayer, not guardian my eyes and ears, and holding on to offenses, and mourning too long.

To come out of all of that I had to begin to do the complete opposite of what I had been doing, one step at a time. I had to create a mental list of successes to lead me to complete wholeness and spiritual freedom. I had to begin to see the good I had left was enough to move forward.

In that, I started to believe that it was enough to be happy again. I needed to be spiritually free because we all know you can be smiling on the outside and still bound inside, you don't know whether you're coming or going. That was me, but because of the steps I took to take the unnecessary things out of my life, I can now smile from the beautiful inner me. My new lean me, no extras, no fat.

I want with all that I am for you to genuinely smile again from the inside. And you will, by God's grace and some practical principles God taught me through my walk with Him. Say with me, "I will smile again, from the inside. " Amen, let's move on.

I said God didn't let me die because he loved me and he sat down in the darkness with me and I saw a glimmer of hope. Well first things first, you have to know having a relationship with Jesus Christ made all the difference in my process of healing. Do you have a relationship with my Lord and Saviour Jesus Christ, if not, will you pray with me today? I promise it'll bless your life. It's very simple, you simply say….

Lord Jesus Come into my life and be my Lord. I believe in my heart and confess with my mouth that you died on the cross and God the Father rose you from the dead on the third day and you are now seated on the right side of the father and reign forevermore.

(Romans 10:9)

And just like that. The heavens are rejoicing. Welcoming you into the family.

Praying the prayer from the previous page, going to a bible teaching church, reading your bible, praying daily, and living through love, you can turn your whole life around before you know it. I know it's easier said than done but it is truly achievable. We've touched on the importance of the checklist now let's delve deeper into the importance of a healthy relationship with God. But first let's get a little self out of the way to clear a path to Jesus.

Everything in our lives is maintained with some type of work. We even sometimes stumble upon possessing things but if we leave them unattended they will slowly deteriorate.

Let's learn more about maintaining what we have, so we don't lose it.

Let it out

This is the lock chapter

A lock is said to be a mechanism for keeping a door, lid, etc., fastened, typically operated only by a key of a particular form. I Chose a lock for this chapter because God is the key that unlocks every door. I just recently had what I call a **locked situation**. I refer to locked situations as times where a series of events lead to a locked moment in your life that releases intense emotions.

The birthday of one of my nearest and dearest deceased siblings came around again a few days before me writing this. Mind you, my son Kevin's picture comes up on my timeline on facebook a few days before this particular date every year. So you know I was already emotional.

My living sister posted a birthday post on facebook and a flood gate opened up. Long story short I ended up crying hysterically. The crying wasn't the surprising thing, it was who was crying. Remember one of my past experiences was a happy child.

How could I be a dysfunctional happy child?

I'll tell you how…

For one, my very nature is to be happy and go lucky, because I grew into a happy go lucky adult and took great offense when someone or something disturbed my happiness. Little did I know that happiness is an emotion. It was really my joy or should I say God's joy that truly was my strength. That unique way I continue to smile in adversity, yep God's joy.

The enemy got in people, places and things over time to take my joy but here I am still standing full of joy. Please know I wasn't always like this, I let the death of my son rob me of my joy because I got tired.

When a person gets tired almost anything can beat them. I can *attest* **(be a witness to; certify formally)** because when everything calmed down after Kevin passed I was well beaten. What could have I done to prevent it?

When I went to treatment in 2020 for my drug addiction I learned about *coping skills* **(methods a person uses to deal with stressful situations)** Coping skills actually do work. I wish I remembered I learned about them in my college Psychology course two years prior to Kevin's death.

In treatment, I just simply practiced things that could relieve stress and cause me to rationalize situations like coloring, drawing, and different projects that *initiated* **(to cause (a process or action) to begin)** confidence and inner strength.

Coping skills are a great way to maintain. Because when you do and say positive things you are clearly not doing and saying negative things.

Being a nice, happy or kind person isn't enough to get through the hard times in life. I learned from my meltdown on my sister's birthday that I'm still that little girl that feels the need to fix what's broken even when I can't. I even wanted to fix the pain experienced, so it would not have ever been felt. But I couldn't fix the pain or the dysfunction then and I certainly can't now and most of the gamechangers have long gone to be with the Lord.

So how does one maintain all They've accomplished with a foundation with cracks in it?

You let it out, unlock that door that has faithfully guarded *repressed* **(of a thought, feeling, or desire) kept suppressed and unconscious in one's mind)** memories, past hurts and *offenses* **(annoyance or resentment brought about by a perceived insult to or disregard for oneself or one's standards or principles)** and right there in that process you will have some hurt but you will begin to heal and God will be there every step of the way. You'll see yourself in ways you've never seen before but most importantly you'll see God in ways you've never seen before.

Like anything holding pressure in, it has to be released or be destroyed. What have you picked up along the way that you are holding on to?

Objects may appear closer

This is the road chapter

A road in this chapter's content is defined as a series of events or a course of action that will lead to a particular outcome. Much like myself, many of you have traveled throughout your life and have picked up a lot of things along the way, you know like souvenirs. I know for me I have found myself hearing people from my past repetitively saying negative things about me like cassette tapes. Even though they're Contrary to what God says about me in His word.

I've even given individuals, for whatever reason, what is not in my power or possession to give,like when someone gives you a gift and you give it away. Life's journey can already be long and hard and if we don't learn that we can't give everyone every part of us we'll give so much of ourselves we won't have enough to freely move forward and reach our destination . This is not God's desire.

Jesus says in John 10:10 of the King James Version **10** The thief cometh not, but for to steal, and to kill, and to destroy: I am come that they might have life, and that they might have it more abundantly.

Abundant life" refers to **life in its abounding fullness of joy and strength for spirit, soul and body.** Our bodies are the vehicles as to how we travel throughout life. We have a mind, which gives us the basic start and know how. Our soul or heart, drives us with passion to pay close attention to signs. And our spirits fuels, maintain, and determine the quality of the trip.

In essence, Our minds form a path as to where we want to go formulated by our surroundings and belief system. Our hearts desire what we are exposed to good or bad and our spirits gauge our conduct as well as our boundaries.

Let's start with our minds, In Philippians 2:5 it says, Let this mind be in you, which was also in Christ Jesus. When you decide to think like Jesus you become clear in vision and purpose. You begin to focus more on doing the will of the father and focusing less on life's distractions.

When all I focused on was being a mother, the death of my son was too much to bear. However When I realized that Kevin was God's and I had been chosen to care for God's child. I then realized God didn't take him from me but indeed brought him back to himself where he started.

In Jeremiah 1:5 (KJV) it reads, Before I formed thee in the belly I knew thee; and before thou camest forth out of the womb I sanctified thee, and I ordained thee a prophet unto the nations.

That means we all started with God and belonged to Him first.

Moving along to the heart of the matter, if I belong to God so do my emotions. Yes that's right our emotions belong to God, that's why God does not want us to operate in our emotions. Anything you purchase is yours and all of its accessories and attachments. And we were bought with a very valuable price on the cross, and that includes us in entirety. It wasn't that God was not allowing me to mourn my son. He just wanted me to do it in a way that served me best and where He gets the glory out of both creations. My son and myself as well.

For one let's clear this up. We do not feel with our hearts in our chest that keep us alive pumping blood throughout our bodies. Please know that when someone breaks our heart it is really our trust and confidence in a preconceived *notion* **(a conception of or belief about something)** Everything that is presented to us goes through a mental process created by upbringings, experiences, memories, and spiritual influences.

More or less the bottom line is this is our soul. It is inclusive of but not limited to our desires, wants, passions...etc. it is the desired prize of the mind and the flesh. Between the two, daily battles take place to win the affection of the heart. To possess and influence it and all it embodies. Who has control of your heart?

Whatever the heart is being influenced by, it gets behind it and drives it. It moves it with such intensity it can change the entire course of one's life. Let me use me as an example... When Kevin passed I was attending a very biblically sound church to attend. I was being fed extremely well, some of the best teaching this side of heaven. Rich food for the soul. However I had been playing cat and mouse with the enemy off and on. I lived in a chaotic environment and I was still quite ignorant concerning a lot of things..

Remember me saying how I sat at Kevin's bedside and envisioned my heart running through my fingers like sand? A clear sign that I felt my heart broken to that degree. And remember I said I lost my hope. I see now but I couldn't see then how my mind or my sound reasoning had begun to lose my soul. The enemy strategically used everything I saw, said and felt and led me to begin to question God much like Eve in the Garden of Eden in the first book of the Bible (Genesis).

My son's death consumed my thoughts, my moves and ultimately my days and there was no room for prayer, worship, and or bible study. My flesh grew strong all the while my spirit grew weak. How was my spirit man to win and I stopped feeding him, no wonder my flesh won that battle. It all unfolded right before my eyes, so why didn't I stop it?

Unavoidable

Purpose

This is the signs chapter

A sign is a gesture or action used to convey information or instructions. Throughout our lives we come across many signs, some good and some bad. Some signs we heed to and some we ignore, some are useful and some aren't. One thing for certain: there will always come a time when a sign is needed in your life.

Like any road, if you drive too far without instruction,you'll get lost and you'll eventually have to stop and reevaluate where you are. When you give yourself to the Lord, God's Spirit comes and dwells in you and helps you travel this road called life. The Holy Spirit is the ultimate GPS. This is important to having a successful life in the Lord. Living for Christ without His Spirit is a straight setup. It is the reason so many believers live powerless lives struggling in the bare necessities like loving one another and forgiveness.

The word of God tells us about our spiritual fight in Ephesians 6:12 For we wrestle not against flesh and blood, but against principalities, against powers, against the ruler of the darkness of this world. Many have no clue who our enemy is exactly. I know I didn't earlier in my life and I am still learning just to what degrees he'll go to destroy me. I walked in a lot of fear worrying about the enemy.

One scripture God led me to was II Corinthians 10:4 For the weapons of our warfare are not carnal but mighty to the pulling down of strong bolds. That clearly tells us that we can't fight a spiritual fight in the flesh or we'll lose every time. This scripture helped my understanding. There was a point where the fights grew more intense and I began getting cocky and growing confident in my own ability. Can you turn to your neighbor and say, "Wrong way!" talking about a very valuable sign.

I was so busy purposely trying to not walk in sin I backed up into it. Remember when I touched on how I made decisions trying to avoid certain falls and still ended up in calamity. I found out that purpose is unavoidable. Whether intentional or by default it will happen.. God's will for your life is undeniable as well as unavoidable.

King David said in Psalm 27 like this Yea though I walk through the valley of shadow of death I will fear no evil cause thou art with me. I learned whether I am led or I lead myself into sinful situations, as long as I choose God to be Lord of my life. I do not have to fear because He is faithful even when I'm not.

He truly knows the way I take.

Remember when you fall, get up, ask for forgiveness, and do your next right thing. Sacrifice momentary pleasure for obedience.

Dead

End

This is the cross chapter

A cross has so many definitions. The meaning that I desire to touch on in this chapter is the one from the crosswalk.com site. It simply says the cross means Love. To me the cross does mean love. It represents Jesus Christ's pain and suffering for my salvation, His father's plan and The Holy Spirits fulfillment. The cross is in itself selfless and sacrificial obedience driven solely by love.

Near the end of my writing this book my closest friend passed away after she succumbed to Sarcoidosis. Her name was Kuipiio T, Livingston. We met in the early 1990's. She was just a teenager, and I was in my early 20's. She was the epitome of a bright light eyed country girl in the big city. Her innocence was intoxicating. For experienced individuals like myself it was refreshingly unbelievable. God had truly kept her for himself.

For As long as I can remember she never exposed the filthiness of disappointment. Test and trial after test and trial she endured and reflected a new amazingly undefiled way of approaching whatever she faced. Don't get me wrong she grew tired many times especially when things happened like her lungs collapsed and the doctors wouldn't stop losing hope in her condition. but when she retreated into God she came back to the fight with fresh eyes even at the end when God told her it was over.

She humbly accepted her savior's comforting words, she didn't want to die but she finished in a graceful nevertheless moment. Leaving many of us speechless echoed by an angelic heavenly standing ovation to a humble soldier that many of us didn't recognize because her armor was love until we eulogized her. God loved through her so perfect, we all felt we were her only object of His affection.

I Traveled to Detroit Michigan for the homegoing one way and returned another way. I purposed in my heart, my hope,and my preconceived notion that when the smoke cleared in my new normal, whatever it may be, I would be strong.

Unlike when my son Kevin passed away from this life, I made specific plans this time based on all I learned and I truly came forth as pure gold after I was tried. I did it yall!!! I won a battle on purpose!!!!

A new normal and I feel strong in my heart, my mind and in my relationship with the Lord. God is so perfect in all of his ways . It took my best sister girl Kuipiio going home to glory for me to grow. I didn't know how much I depended on her until I had to get on that plane back to St Louis without her in my world.

I had no choice but to put on my big girl panties (as she would say) and accomplish what I set out to do. And that was Come back strong and I did. I came back stronger and it was because God was with me every step of the way rooting me on. God raised believers up to sow words of wisdom in my life. The Holy Spirit brought back the word of

God to my remembrance. God was everything I needed, when I needed Him. From the beginning to the end.

God loved me so much to have Kuipiio in my life for over 25 years, however I learned more from her in the last year of her life than over the course of our lives together. And I want to share it with you….

Here goes…. Our lives can have more mistakes than we care to remember but it's the end of a man or woman that matters the most. We're all living and moving to an unavoidable end, there's no choices after heaven or hell, So please, My Loves choose life while you can and let's get out there and live the part of our lives that matter the most. A life of sharing the love of Jesus Christ.

Saying all of that I'll leave you with my final letter to one of my greatest inspirations

Kuipiio Tinishia Livingston (March 9, 1976- September 30, 2021)

Letter to My Kuipiio,

Kuip…. Kuip…. Kuip…..

Not gone but asleep

Baby Sister. You were famous!!!

I didn't know

I was too busy hoarding you

And how you loved me so.

I look at the love you've shown

others In our Chitlin circuit

Your infectious smile Noone'll forget it

You walked with big wigs and sang for them all.

The grandest of the grand, the smallest of the small.

You spread your wisdom likes seeds to be thrown

Very careful who they landed on

Every word you spoke was well thought

Many heard but few caught

Filled with Grace your every step

Received secrets one every kept.

I could forever go on and on

About how at times we truly were one

No greater you I'll know again

My closest you My closest friend

So I'll digress with what you gave me

When people ask I'll say Kuip made me

Made me do all she told

because it took you dying, for me to grow….

Thank you SISTER Thank you FRIEND

This is my beginning and not your end

Your love in my heart I'll forever keep

Kuip…. Kuip…. Kuip…. Not gone asleep.

As you were, My little Angel…. First Lady

A FINAL NOTE FROM
THE FIRST LADY….

It is my prayer that whenever life becomes a little too hard to bear, you look back through this book and it helps guide you through your storm, Whatever that may be.

I pray it is used as a useful tool for generations to come. That it saves, heals and sets free in homes, institutions and on street corners. I pray it is the water of life that can maneuver in every crack and crevice of darkness to reach the farthest reaches of souls and that God be glorified in each life touched.

I challenge you, **My Loves….**

focus, begin again, fill in your four dots and win.

As you were…. First Lady 💋

Until
Our
Next
Read

*Note*First Lady Tee lent herself to these lessons for you….

ABOUT THE AUTHOR....

Tina Louise Mitchell was born to Pastor Wilson Jemison and Missionary Lattie Mae Sanders. The youngest of all her siblings, Tina had big dreams from a young age to be an aspiring author. Alongside her husband Bishop Milano T. Mitchell, First Lady has taken up her cross and her pen in hopes of writing herself as well as all of her brothers and sisters in the faith free from bondage.